Color Your Own
CLASSIC MOVIE POSTERS
RENDERED BY MARTY NOBLE

DOVER PUBLICATIONS, INC.
MINEOLA, NEW YORK

NOTE

This collection of vintage movie posters, ranging from the silent film era to the 1960s, includes thirty of the most beloved motion pictures of all time. Unforgettable characters, compelling scenes, and star-studded casts all blend together to make a film memorable, relegating it a treasured place in cinematic history. Represented here are authentic posters from iconic movies such as *Casablanca*, *The Wizard of Oz*, *High Noon*, and *Gone with the Wind*. With this handsome coloring book, movie audiences and colorists alike can truly appreciate these posters as stellar pieces of artwork.

All thirty of the movie posters in this book are shown in full color on the inside front and back covers. Use this color scheme as a guide to create your own version of a classic poster or change the colors to see the effects of mood and tone. Captions identify the title of the film and its original release date.

Copyright

Copyright © 2006 by Dover Publications, Inc.
All rights reserved.

Bibliographical Note

Color Your Own Classic Movie Posters is a new work, first published by
Dover Publications, Inc., in 2006.

International Standard Book Number

ISBN-13: 978-0-486-44812-1
ISBN-10: 0-486-44812-6

Manufactured in the United States by LSC Communications
44812613   2020
www.doverpublications.com

1. Blood and Sand (1922)

2. Robin Hood (1922)

3. The Gold Rush (1925)

4. The Phantom of the Opera (1925)

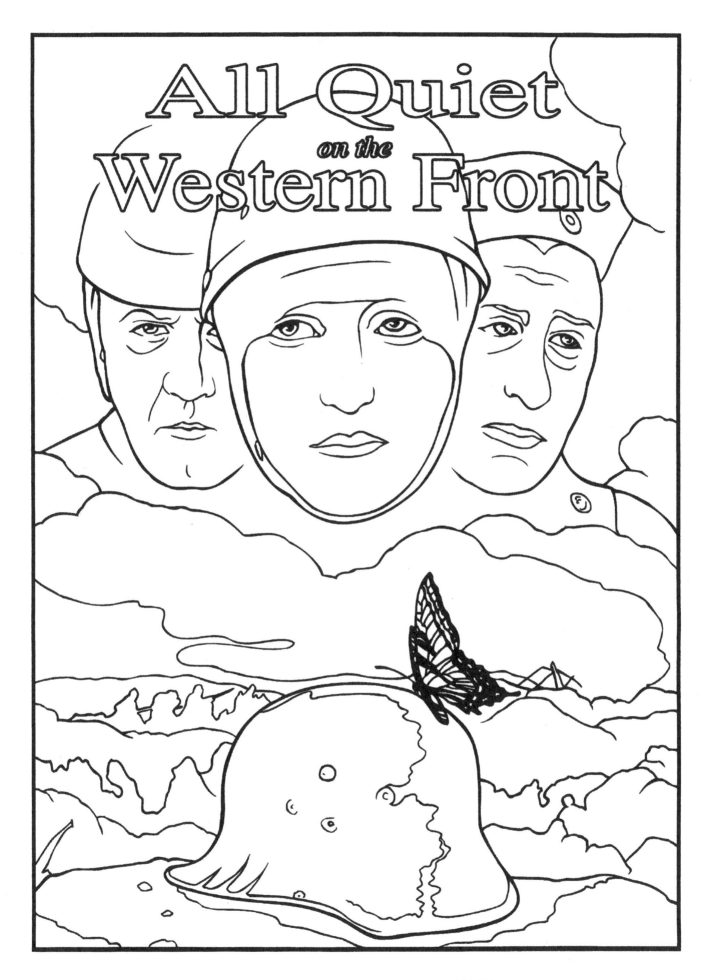

5. All Quiet on the Western Front (1930)

6. Frankenstein (1931)

7. Duck Soup (1933)

8. King Kong (1933)

9. It Happened One Night (1934)

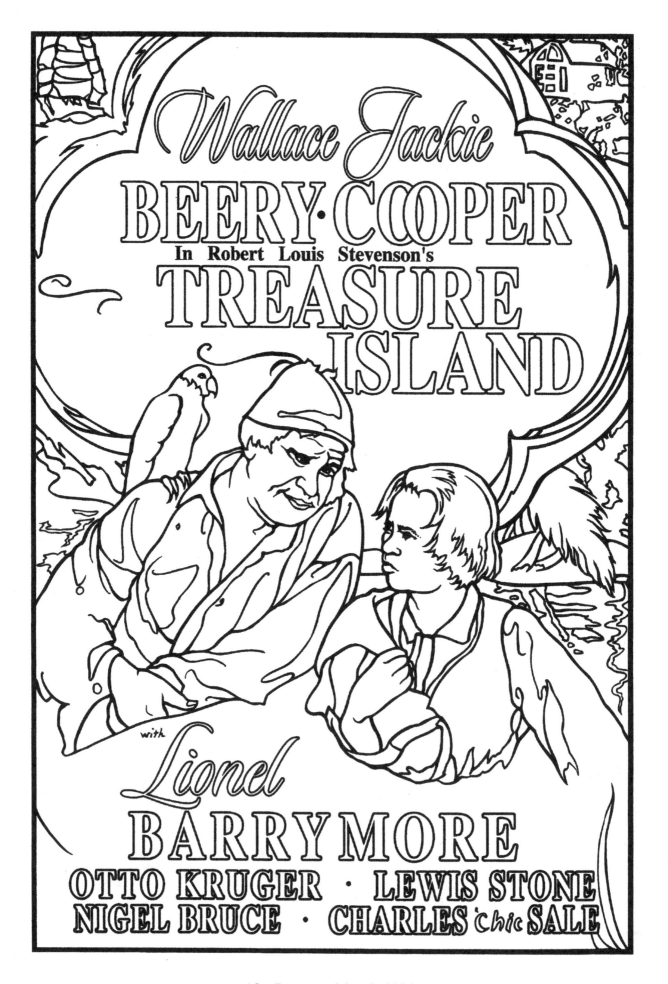

10. *Treasure Island* (1934)

11. Captain January (1936)

12. Gone with the Wind (1939)

13. Stagecoach (1939)

14. The Wizard of Oz (1939)

15. Citizen Kane (1941)

16. *Shadow of the Thin Man* (1941)

17. Casablanca (1942)

18. It's a Wonderful Life (1946)

19. The Asphalt Jungle (1950)

20. The African Queen (1951)

21. An American in Paris (1951)

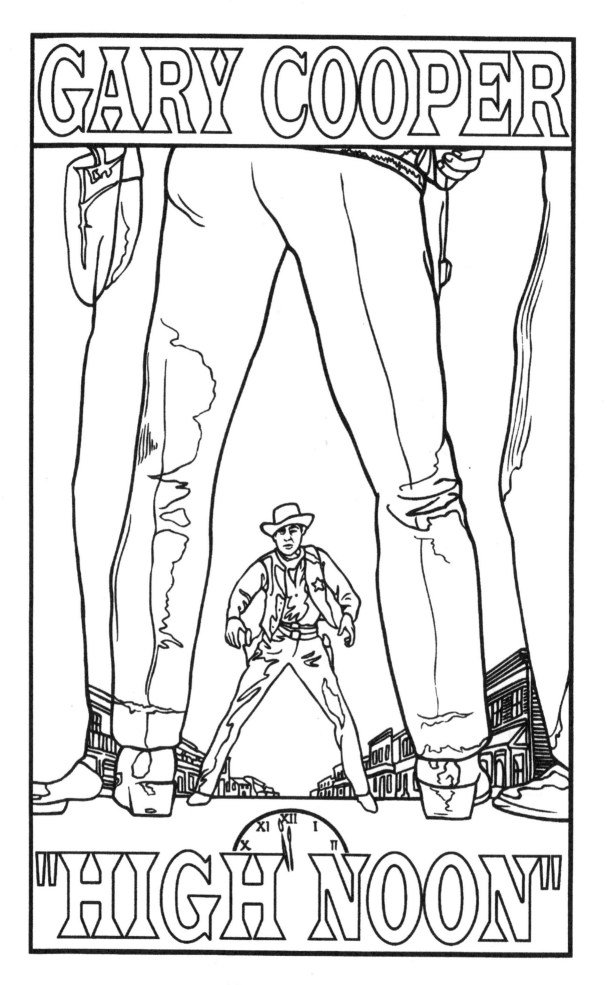

22. High Noon (1952)

23. Singin' in the Rain (1952)

24. Rear Window (1954)

25. Forbidden Planet (1956)

26. Giant (1956)

27. Ben-Hur (1959)

28. North by Northwest (1959)

29. Breakfast at Tiffany's (1961)

30. West Side Story (1961)